@RosenTeenTalk

SETTING AND RESPECTING BOUNDARIES

Lorraine Harrison

ROSEN PUBLISHING

Published in 2026 by The Rosen Publishing Group, Inc.
2544 Clinton Street, Buffalo, NY 14224

First Edition

Editor: Katie Kawa
Designer: Michael Flynn

Photo Credits: Cover pp. 1, 3, 5, 45 TimeImage Production; cover (emoji) Cosmic_Design/Shutterstock.com; cover and interior (phone) Vitya_M/Shutterstock.com; pp. 3, 14 BearFotos/Shutterstock.com; pp. 3, 25, 38 Monkey Business Images/Shutterstock.com; pp. 3, 35 Prostock-studio/Shutterstock.com; p. 7 Bits And Splits/Shutterstock.com; p. 8 KANGWANS/Shutterstock.com; p. 11 Daniel Hoz/Shutterstock.com; p. 12 lemono/Shutterstock.com; p. 13 Helder Almeida/Shutterstock.com; p. 17 DimaBerlin/Shutterstock.com; p. 18 Anatoliy Karlyuk/Shutterstock.com; p. 19 Drazen Zigic/Shutterstock.com; p. 20 Golden Pixels LLC/Shutterstock.com; p. 21 evrymmnt/Shutterstock.com; p. 23 Monkey Business Images/Shutterstock.com; p. 26 Chimpinski/Shutterstock.com; p. 27 William Perugini/Shutterstock.com; p. 29 Iren_Geo/Shutterstock.com; p. 30 mentalmind/Shutterstock.com; p. 31 Daniel M Ernst/Shutterstock.com; p. 32 Inside Creative House/Shutterstock.com; p. 33 F01 PHOTO/Shutterstock.com; p. 37 pikselstock/Shutterstock.com; p. 39 Dasha Petrenko/Shutterstock.com; p. 40 Ariya J/Shutterstock.com; p. 41 fizkes/Shutterstock.com; p. 43 Frame Stock Footage/Shutterstock.com.

Cataloging-in-Publication Data

Names: Harrison, Lorraine.
Title: Setting and respecting boundaries / Lorraine Harrison.
Description: Buffalo, NY : Rosen Publishing, 2026. | Series: @RosenTeenTalk | Includes glossary and index.
Identifiers: ISBN 9781499479997 (pbk.) | ISBN 9781725342460 (library bound) | ISBN 9781725342477 (ebook)
Subjects: LCSH: Boundaries (Psychology). Self-protective behavior. | Interpersonal relations--Psychological aspects.
Classification: LCC BF697.5 H37 2026 | DDC 155.2--dc2

Manufactured in the United States of America

CPSIA Compliance Information: Batch #CWRYA26. For Further Information contact Rosen Publishing at 1-800-237-9932.

CONTENTS

Chapter 1

What Are Boundaries?

I've been dating Jaxson for a few weeks now, and things are going really great. I love holding his hand, and he even gave me my first kiss after our date last Friday!

Kissing Jaxson was amazing, and I love being around him. But sometimes I get nervous about doing more than just kissing. Does he want that? Will he be mad if I tell him I just want to kiss for now?

I talked to my older sister about what I was feeling. She told me that I should set some boundaries with Jaxson about what I want and don't want to do. I know that's a good idea, but it makes me a little nervous. What if I hurt his feelings?

Boundaries can be an uncomfortable thing to talk about. However, they're very important!

BOUNDARY BASICS

Boundaries exist all around us. For example, property boundaries, or property lines, mark the limits of someone's land. If that boundary isn't respected and someone crosses the line, there are often **consequences**.

The same is true for a person's boundaries. They mark the limits of what a person considers acceptable treatment. This means boundaries are clear statements of how we want to be treated. They draw a line between what we will and won't accept. Often, healthy boundaries also include a clear statement of what we'll do if someone crosses that line.

WHAT WE CAN CONTROL

Some people believe boundaries are for trying to control someone else's behavior, or actions. But we can't control other people. We can only control ourselves. Healthy boundaries aren't about trying to make another person do what you want. Instead, they're about how you **respond** to the behavior of other people. You can't change other people. However, you can change how you allow yourself to be treated. You can set a boundary and step back from someone who hurts your feelings or makes you feel unsafe.

KINDS OF BOUNDARIES

Boundaries can be used in many areas of your life. Physical boundaries deal with how you do and don't want to be touched by another person. These can also include boundaries that deal with personal space.

These are just some of the kinds of boundaries people set.

Emotional boundaries deal with how you share your feelings and how you're treated when you do. Material boundaries deal with things, such as money and clothes, you are and aren't willing to share with other people. Time boundaries deal with how you want to spend your time.

EXAMPLES OF BOUNDARIES

BOUNDARY	DEALS WITH	EXAMPLE
physical	touching and personal space	"I don't feel comfortable hugging Dad's coworker. I'll shake his hand instead."
emotional	when and how much you share about your feelings	"If you continue to tease me when I cry, I'll stop sharing my feelings with you because I don't feel supported."
material	money and other things you are and aren't willing to share with others	"I am trying to save money for a car, so I can't go out to dinner with you every weekend."
time	how you spend your time and who you spend it with	"My grades are important to me, so on nights before a test, I can't stay late at your house."
sexual	what you are and aren't comfortable doing, talking about, or hearing about when it comes to sex	"I don't feel ready to have sex. If you don't stop when I say no, I will leave."
intellectual	thoughts, beliefs, and opinions	"I don't want to talk about the news when we eat dinner because it upsets me. If you continue to talk about it, I'll eat in another room."

HOW DO BOUNDARIES HELP?

Sometimes setting boundaries means having hard conversations, or talks. However, taking care of yourself is worth the effort.

When we set boundaries, we honor our values—what's important to us. Setting healthy boundaries, which are created with care, can help you feel safe. They can also keep you from feeling burned out or resentful about how others are treating you.

Boundaries can also make **relationships** stronger. They build trust, create open **communication**, and allow both people in a relationship to have their needs met.

Fast Fact!

A study that came out in 2024 showed that 27 percent of U.S. teens are dealing with burnout.

Writing in a journal can be a great way to explore your values and needs in order to set healthy boundaries for yourself.

BOUNDARIES AND BURNOUT

Setting healthy boundaries can help protect you from burnout. When you're burned out, you often feel tired and hopeless. Sometimes you might even feel numb, or unable to feel anything. Burnout can also cause problems with sleep, stomach problems, and headaches. Burnout sometimes happens when people do so much for others that they forget to care for themselves. Healthy boundaries can help you find the time and energy for self-care.

A TWO-WAY STREET

Boundaries aren't just for you, though. Everyone has the ability to set boundaries. This means people might sometimes set a boundary with you. Your friend might tell you they won't hang out with you as much if you keep putting down their ideas. Your boyfriend might say he can't text you after 10 p.m. because he needs to sleep.

It doesn't always feel good when someone sets a boundary with us. However, it's important to respect those boundaries anyway.

You're allowed to set boundaries that honor your needs, and other people are allowed to do the same.

Chapter 2

Boundaries in Families

"You're grounded!"

My dad's voice was the first thing I heard when I got home. I was a few minutes later than my 10 p.m. **curfew**, but I didn't know I'd get grounded for it.

"Jordan's mom was late picking us up," I tried to explain. "And I don't get why it's such a big deal anyway."

My dad took a deep breath. "Because when you're not home by the time we'd agreed on, I get worried that something bad happened to you."

"I get it," I said. "But I wish you would have told me that being grounded was the consequence for breaking curfew." I knew why my dad was upset. I just wish he'd been clearer in the first place.

Curfews are a kind of boundary that parents sometimes set with their children.

PARENTS HAVE BOUNDARIES TOO

Parents are people too! And that means parents sometimes need to set boundaries with their kids. A curfew is one example of this kind of boundary. Another might be asking for everyone to stay off their phones during family dinners. Other boundaries set by parents might deal with how their kids speak to them.

The best kinds of boundaries are ones that are clearly communicated. It's helpful for parents to explain why they're setting a boundary. It's also helpful for them to communicate the consequences of disrespecting a boundary.

Sometimes it can be hard to remember that your parents have their own needs, but they do. Everyone does!

ASKING QUESTIONS

Healthy boundaries allow for more open communication. This can be true for parents and their kids too. For example, it's OK to ask questions about a boundary your parents or guardians have set. It's also OK to ask for them to clearly explain the consequences of crossing a boundary. They might not give you an answer—or an answer you think is fair—but it's important to talk about boundaries as a family so everyone is on the same page.

TOO MUCH TOGETHERNESS

Boundaries involving physical touch are important in families. Not everyone likes hugs or kisses. If you don't, it's OK to set a boundary with your family members and tell them you'd rather shake their hand or give them a fist bump instead.

It's also important to respect family members who have set this kind of boundary with you. For example, your cousin might say she doesn't want anyone kissing her new baby. That's a boundary you can respect to make her feel more comfortable.

Some **cultures** value family over everything else. In these cultures, it can be hard to set boundaries with family members. However, if you feel uncomfortable or unsafe around a family member, it's important to talk to a trusted adult about boundaries that can help you feel better.

WORDS MATTER

An important boundary to respect—with family members, friends, or anyone else—is related to pronouns. People will sometimes let you know what pronouns to use when talking to and about them. For example, they might say their pronouns are "she/her" or "they/them" and they don't want anyone to use other pronouns to describe them. Respecting this boundary shows respect for the person who set it. This is a boundary you can set with others too.

TAKING TEASING TOO FAR

In many families, teasing is seen as a sign of love. Not everyone feels this way, though. If teasing makes you feel uncomfortable, it's OK to tell the person or people doing it to stop.

An example of a boundary around teasing might be: "I don't like being teased about my hair. If you continue to do it, I'm going to go watch TV in another room." The teasing might not stop, but you can choose to respect yourself and leave the **situation**.

Setting healthy boundaries with family members can keep you from resenting them, or being upset with them because you feel they're not doing what they should be doing.

TOUGH TOPICS

Families don't always agree about everything happening in the world. These differences in opinions can sometimes lead to big fights. For this reason, some people set boundaries about what they will and won't talk about or listen to at family gatherings. You could say, "I don't feel comfortable talking about **politics** with our whole family. If people start arguing about it, I will leave the room until it cools down." This is a way to protect your peace without trying to control others.

SHARING ON SOCIAL MEDIA

Your family members probably enjoy sharing things about their family on social media. This might include stories about you or pictures or videos of you.

You're allowed to have a say in the kind of content that's shared about you online. Social media boundaries are important! This might mean setting boundaries with your parents about what kinds of stories you're comfortable having them share. It might also mean setting boundaries with your siblings about sharing **embarrassing** pictures or videos.

Some people share their whole lives online, including pictures or videos of their children. Others, however, set boundaries around what they will and won't share when it comes to their kids.

Chapter 3

Boundaries with Friends

I used to love spending time with Brooklyn. She's been my best friend since we were in first grade. Lately, though, hanging out with her is exhausting.

Brooklyn started hanging out with some new girls, and they love to party. I've gone to a couple of their parties with Brooklyn, and each time, she tries to get me to drink. I don't want to, and I've told her that. But what I want doesn't seem to matter.

So I decided I have to talk to her before we go out tonight. I'm going to tell her that I don't want to be teased for not drinking, and if she can't let it go, I'm not going to any more parties with her.

Setting boundaries with friends can be hard. However, real friends will respect your boundaries and treat you how you want to be treated.

STAYING SAFE

Some of the most important boundaries you can set with your friends involve alcohol and other drugs. If being around alcohol or other drugs makes you feel uncomfortable or unsafe, you can set a boundary to avoid situations where drinking or drug use will be taking place.

It's also very important to set clear boundaries around drinking, drug use, and driving. Letting friends—and family members—know that you won't be getting in a car with them if they've been drinking or using drugs is a boundary that can save your life.

Fast Fact!

In 2023, 1,392 people under the age of 21 died in car crashes involving a drunk driver.

Boundaries often exist to keep us safe. For example, if you don't think someone is a safe driver, you can let your friends know that you won't be getting in a car with that person.

FOR MORE INFORMATION

If you want to know more about setting healthy boundaries with your friends when it comes to alcohol and other drugs, these books can help:

- Benac, Eric. *Peer Pressure to Smoke or Vape: Finding the Strength in You.* Broomall, PA: Mason Crest Publishers, 2021.
- Bongiorno, Elissa. *I Got Caught Drinking and Driving ... What's Next?* Buffalo, NY: Rosen Publishing, 2022.
- McKinney, Donna B. *Substance Addiction.* Minneapolis, MN: Essential Library, 2022.

YOU CAN'T FIX EVERYTHING

Friends are often the people we go to when we need to talk about our feelings. However, sometimes friends have problems that need more **serious** attention than we can give.

If you have a friend who's dealing with serious problems at home, in their dating life, or with their **mental** health, it's not your job to fix things. It's OK to set a boundary with them. You can suggest that they talk to a trusted adult or a mental health **professional** instead of or in addition to talking to you.

Some friends might expect you to text them back as soon as they send you a message. It can be helpful to set a boundary with these friends. You can explain that you'll text them back when you have the time and energy to give them a thoughtful reply.

"I" STATEMENTS

When setting boundaries with friends, family, or anyone else, it's helpful to use "I" statements. These are sentences that **focus** on your feelings and why you're setting a boundary. They don't put the blame on the other person. You might want to say, "You never listen to me." However, it's more helpful to say, "I feel like I'm not being heard." "I" statements are a way to make hard conversations a little easier.

MENTAL HEALTH MATTERS

Friendship isn't always easy. This is especially true if you're dealing with a lot of **stress** at school or at home. And it can be even harder if you're dealing with mental illnesses such as depression or anxiety.

If things your friends talk about start to **affect** your mental health, it's OK to let them know. It's also OK to ask for some alone time. Boundaries exist to help your mental health. Just remember to communicate them clearly and kindly.

Your friends can also set boundaries with you. When this happens, it's important to remember that you're not being **punished**. Your friend is just trying to take care of themselves.

MAKING IT EASIER

Setting boundaries can be uncomfortable, but there are things you can do to make it easier. For example, you can choose to communicate a boundary at the right time. The middle of a fight is not the right time to set a boundary with someone. It's best to have that conversation when everyone is calm.

It can also be helpful to practice what you're going to say ahead of time. This can help you speak with confidence, or belief in yourself.

It's often helpful to talk about boundaries in person instead of through texts or DMs. Miscommunication can happen when you can't see someone's body language or hear the tone in their voice.

WHEN SOMEONE SETS A BOUNDARY WITH YOU

Learning to respect someone's boundaries is just as important as learning to set your own. If someone sets a boundary with you, it's OK to feel a little confused, upset, or hurt at first. However, take a deep breath, and don't take things personally. Ask questions if you need to make things clearer, but don't push back or try to change their mind. "No" is a complete sentence, and everyone's boundaries deserve respect.

Chapter 4

BOUNDARIES AND DATING

Boundaries are a way to honor what matters to you. That's especially important when you're dating someone. It can be easy to lose yourself in a relationship. When you really like someone, you can start to care more about what matters to them than what matters to you.

Setting boundaries early on in a relationship is a good way to let the person you're dating know your values. It gives them a chance to see who you really are and helps you stay true to yourself.

It's normal to want to make the person you're dating happy. However, your happiness matters too!

BOUNDARIES AND CONSENT

Setting clear physical boundaries early in a relationship allows both people to be comfortable and safe with each other. It lets both people know what's acceptable and what the limits are when dealing with kissing, touching, and other kinds of physical **affection**.

A helpful boundary to set in relationships involves consent, which is the act of saying yes to something. You might set a boundary that you will not kiss or touch the person you're dating without clear consent—and that you expect the same.

One of the most important boundaries in a relationship is "No means no." If the person you're dating says "no" to something you want to do physically, don't try to do it anyway.

BOUNDARIES CAN CHANGE

Boundaries don't always stay the same forever. For example, early in a relationship, someone might set the boundary that they don't want the person they're dating to come to their house. However, as they get more comfortable in the relationship, they might change that boundary and allow the other person to come over. In some cases, though, boundaries don't change. You shouldn't expect someone's boundaries to change without them saying so.

TIME FOR EVERYONE

When you're dating someone, you usually want to spend as much time with them as you can. However, you shouldn't ignore the other people and **responsibilities** in your life because you're in a relationship. This is where boundaries with time can be very helpful.

You might need to tell the person you're dating that Friday nights are family nights, so you can't go out then. Or they might tell you that they can't text you when they're at lacrosse practice.

Setting clear boundaries around your time can help your friendships stay strong even when you're dating someone.

A WARNING SIGN

If someone you're dating doesn't respect your boundaries, that could be a warning sign of abusive behavior. One in three teens in the United States has been abused by someone they're dating. Abuse generally means harm, and that harm can be physical, sexual, or emotional. If you're noticing warning signs of an abusive partner or have experienced abuse, talk to a trusted adult. They can get you the help you need.

PEOPLE PLEASING

If you have a very hard time setting boundaries, you might be a people pleaser. A people pleaser is someone who always wants others to be happy—even if that means ignoring their own happiness and needs.

Learning to set healthy boundaries is important for people pleasers. It allows them to practice saying that they have needs and that those needs are important. This is especially important for girls and women, because they're the group most likely to be people pleasers.

Fast Fact!

According to a 2024 study, more than half of all women in the United States think of themselves as people pleasers.

Many women say they were taught to be people pleasers. Learning to set boundaries now can help you teach the next **generation** something healthier.

FOR MORE INFORMATION

If you're looking for more advice on how to set boundaries, you can check out these websites:

- Boundaries: What They Are and How to Create Them: *wellnesscenter.uic.edu/news-stories/boundaries-what-are-they-and-how-to-create-them/*
- Consent 101: Respect, Boundaries, and Building Trust: *rainn.org/share-the-facts/consent-101-respect-boundaries-and-building-trust/*
- How to Set Healthy Boundaries: *www.wondermind.com/article/setting-boundaries/*

HOW TO HANDLE IT

Even if you're not a people pleaser, setting boundaries can still be hard. Most people do whatever they can to avoid feeling uncomfortable, and boundaries can be uncomfortable to talk about.

However, uncomfortable doesn't mean impossible. You can handle hard conversations and do hard things. You can start small and practice around people you trust before you move on to harder conversations. Boundaries are a sign of respect—for yourself and for others—and that respect is worth some hard work.

Setting boundaries can make some people feel very anxious. A therapist can teach you **coping** skills to work through your anxiety and have hard conversations.

PROFESSIONAL HELP

If you have a really hard time setting boundaries, it might be helpful to talk to a mental health professional, often called a therapist, about it. Therapists can help those who are people pleasers learn to advocate, or stand up, for their needs. They can also help you practice setting boundaries in a safe space before you set them with other people in your life. Seeing a therapist is a good way to take care of your mental health.

On the Same Page

I knew I needed to talk to Jaxson about how far I was ready to go in our relationship. I wrote in my journal about what felt right and what didn't, so I knew what to say the next time we hung out.

The time came when Jaxson and I had just finished playing video games in his basement. He went to kiss me, but I stopped him. I took a deep breath and told him that I like kissing him, but that's all I want to do right now.

"I feel the same way!" Jaxson said. "In fact, I was worried you wanted more. So I'm really glad you told me."

I was so happy! It feels great to be on the same page.

Taking care of yourself by setting boundaries allows you to take better care of others too.

GLOSSARY

affect: To produce an effect on something.

affection: Care and love.

communication: The use of words, sounds, signs, or behaviors to convey ideas, thoughts, and feelings.

consequence: Something important that happens because of an action or set of conditions.

cope: To try to manage with some success.

culture: A group of people who share the same beliefs and ways of life.

curfew: The requirement that someone be home by a certain time.

embarrassing: Causing a feeling of foolishness.

focus: To direct attention or effort at something.

generation: A group of people born and living during the same time.

mental: Relating to the mind.

politics: Activities and opinions that relate to governments.

professional: A person who does a job that requires special education or skill.

punish: To make someone suffer for doing something wrong.

relationship: The way in which two or more people are connected.

respond: To do something as a reaction to something that has happened.

responsibility: A duty that a person should do.

serious: Causing worry or harm.

situation: All the facts, conditions, and events that affect someone or something in a certain time and place.

stress: Something that causes strong feelings of worry.

INDEX